D0941136

THE SWAN

DISCARD

The Swan

THE STORY OF ANNA PAVLOVA
BY HELEN MAY

Illustrated by Peggy Fortnum

THOMAS NELSON AND SONS LTD EDINBURGH

THOMAS NELSON AND SONS LTD
Parkside Works Edinburgh 9
36 Park Street London W1
312 Flinders Street Melbourne C1

302–304 Barclays Bank Building
Commissioner and Kruis Streets
Johannesburg

THOMAS NELSON AND SONS (CANADA) LTD
91–93 Wellington Street West Toronto 1

THOMAS NELSON AND SONS
19 East 47th Street New York 17

SOCIÉTÉ FRANÇAISE D'EDITIONS NELSON
97 rue Monge Paris 5

———

© Helen May 1958

J
921
P338M
c-1

Printed in Great Britain by
Thomas Nelson and Sons Ltd, Edinburgh

COUNTY LIBRARY
DISCARD
TILLAMOOK, ORE.

I

HOW can one sketch a sunset in black and white? It is all colour.

Those who saw Pavlova remember colour, rich and glowing with life. Pavlova *was* life—colour and rhythm and life.

'When you do dance, I wish you a wave o' th' sea, that you might ever do nothing but that'—as Shakespeare's Florizel, in the play, *The Winter's Tale*, visualised his Perdita, so did Pavlova dance, for she had, as Cecchetti (her professor) admitted, ' that which can only be taught by God '.

Why is it, among a hundred photographs of the Ballet, that a portrait of Pavlova always conveys a sense of peace—and this when she herself was the most vivid dancer of them all ? Here is not the glamour of the flesh, but rather the ecstasy of the spirit, and the sight of this now in a hurried ungracious world gives us a moment of tranquillity.

The wonder of Pavlova was never that her dancing

appeared so very difficult, but that it seemed so surprisingly easy. She led the life of an artist in a contemplative sense, content in her humble surroundings.

Born in Leningrad (St Petersburg as it was then called, in the days when it was still a Royal city), her parents were quite simple folk. Neither of them had been dancers themselves, and the mother must have had a hard struggle, for her little daughter was but two years old when her husband died. Anna was her only child, and this doubtless drew them closer in affection.

For six years there appears to have been no sign of the great gifts the child possessed. Early photographs show her as a quiet, earnest mite, a dreamy expression generally on her face, with no hint of the fire that burned within.

The family were of Polish origin, like that other genius, Chopin, the famous composer. Perhaps that accounts for much: the same poetic melancholy and the great vitality. It is characteristic of the Poles' temperament, as shown in their national dances. Similar moods are evident in Scottish dancing, a comparison that Pavlova herself alluded to. She was ever what the Scots call 'fey'. In her real-life outlook on the world a delightful vein of fantasy showed at unexpected moments.

Phyllis Bedells in her book, *My Dancing Days*, tells how Pavlova often came to tea with her, and once, as she was

rushing out into the garden, some flowing drapery on her dress caught on a rose-tree and broke off a branch. Real tears streamed down Pavlova's face, and never ceased until the branch had been grafted together again.

Again, in Mr Dandré's (he was her husband) *Life of Pavlova* he tells how once a favourite bird of hers flew away. Madame was very sad, but it returned and she took it to bed with her.

When he entered the room it was to see a little figure sitting up amid pillows with the wayward bird nestling against her cheek, just as though it were really telling her about the adventure !

It will be understood how, as flowers and birds were her friends, she *felt* their small lives, so that it was little marvel that she portrayed them so movingly in her solo dances.

But all this was in the years to come. Now she still lived

4

quietly, serenely enjoying the beauties of Nature and the things of Nature when she was taken into the country, and so might it have continued ; but when she was eight years old, as a special treat mother took her to see *The Sleeping Princess*— and her future was settled.

That performance, her first sight of *real* ballet, stirred her so vastly that she knew what she must be ; not merely what she wished to be, for that wish had scarcely been born, but what she *must* be. With large dark eyes opened wide she suddenly saw, saw it all, and there vowed that one day she too would dance *The Sleeping Princess* on the stage.

In all the hours of practice it must have seemed long years until that time came, but she waited, watched and worked with her gaze fixed on that point.

After much begging her mother finally took her to the school run by the State, and after a strict examination, both physical and mental, the small enthusiast was accepted.

This famous academy was a

5

wonderful institution in which the Czar of Russia took the greatest interest, granting invaluable aid in money and patronage. The Imperial Ballet School, of which one can learn all in the dancer Karsavina's book, *Theatre Street*, was somewhat like a large boarding-school for boys and girls, the chief difference being that, apart from some general education, knowledge of the Ballet and its allied Arts was the main subject.

The little Anna must have felt bewildered at first to find herself suddenly in the rush and bustle of a big city, St Petersburg, after the restful peace of her green fields.

Then too, the occasional visit of her mother—all that was permitted—was the sole link with her former home.

Many tears were doubtless shed, and doubtless soon forgotten, when she was again practising her beloved dancing, for no personal troubles could shake that firm resolve to become eventually a dancer. Neither frail physique nor a tendency to poor health must stop that.

The teachers were distressed at Anna's thinness, and she was put on a special diet and made to take cod-liver oil, which she thought horrid, although it is doubtful if she really noticed, for all she ever saw was the Dance.

Like the young Nelson's perpetual sea-sickness which never stopped his going to sea, so with Anna Pavlova, all the distracting commotion of the life into which she had rashly introduced herself was as nothing to her great aim.

Among the many boys and girls, with all their noisy frolics, there must have been trials to an only child, but Anna was not disturbed, for her dancing was a thing apart and above her associates. Popular though she was on account of her warm-hearted and generous nature, it was Anna's ship she was sailing and no-one else's oar would ever turn her course.

Thoroughness down to the minutest detail was her keynote.

' Genius is the capacity for taking infinite pains ' and ' Dogged does it ' are two popular sayings which Pavlova proved to be true. Cod-liver oil, pale cheeks, aching muscles—these were nothing, for Anna Pavlova the Ballerina was being made.

Since that day when her life can truly be said to have begun, when with *The Sleeping Princess* she opened her eyes to a new world, her determination had steadily grown, and while still in her teens she appeared as a Soloist, being most favourably noticed by all those who mattered in the world of Ballet. Instinctively the real ' balletomanes ' sensed that in Anna Pavlova there was a difference, some finer spark, and that her future must be carefully watched and jealously guarded, to bring out all the subtlety her work promised. What a thrill she must have felt to know that all those grilling

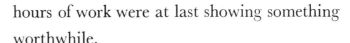

hours of work were at last showing something worthwhile.

What a brilliant spectacle the Theatre must have been that night, too, with the rich Russian aristocracy in Court dress : gay and colourful uniforms contrasting dashingly with the gleaming pastel satins of the women's evening gowns. Crystal chandeliers catching the rainbow lights in the diamond tiaras, dancing sparkle everywhere — including the eyes of Pavlova. . . .

Well, it was another milestone passed : Pavlova had 'arrived'.

There was still a long way to go, and many difficulties were ahead of her—difficult decisions to be made—but, being a genius, she surmounted difficulties more quickly than others, and the confidence that this success gave her added energy to master technical difficulties, so that those who knew marvelled at her rapid advance.

The poor little Russian girl was now an acknowledged personality in the theatre of the dance. Anna Pavlova had 'found her feet'—those wonderful feet that would carry her how many miles before they danced away with her . . . ?

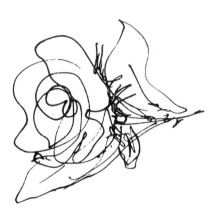

2

It was truly a 'galaxy' that was displayed at that home of Ballet, St Petersburg : all the glittering stars of the Czarist times, the many fabulous 'ballerina assoluta' (the highest rank attainable) with their palaces and jewels. Yet to the more discerning the simple, earnest Pavlova stood out.

Undoubtedly the peak of Classical Ballet had been attained then, with superb dancers, master musicians—Tchaikovsky,

Delibes, Drigo—all composing such danceable melodies, expert choreographers with the great Petipa leading. . . .

All that was possibly lagging behind was the décor. Scenic artists had reached the limit in pantomime-like invention of the ' transformation ' scene type, but the net result was largely a glorification of the ' penny plain and tuppence coloured ' picture, neither true to real life nor genuinely imaginative. Here were outmoded ideas, and as such not fit for the living Theatre.

A small coterie of progressive theatre artists, whose work had been based on study in Museums, Picture Galleries,

Concert Halls and Libraries rather than the humdrum routine of ballet technique, deplored this stagnant state, among them Alexandre Benois, later to be the virtual creator of that masterpiece *Petrouchka*.

This circle of friends strove for a new and more advanced approach in keeping with the twentieth century, which had recently dawned. They saw in Pavlova a freshness and freedom that was their ideal, and soon, under the leadership of that superlative organiser, Serge de Diaghilev, was formed a Russian Ballet that was later to make history and be remembered probably for all time.

It was a courageous undertaking for all concerned when Diaghilev's Ballet Russe announced its world première at the Théâtre Chantilly, Paris. Huge posters of Pavlova in *Les*

Sylphides heralded a success gigantic beyond hope or expectation. Presenting an amalgamation of the Arts such as the sphere of ballet had never before shown, the impact on the art public of Paris, and subsequently London, was overwhelming. Small wonder, when in one single performance was presented the best music, painters and dancers of the world, not forgetting the choreography of Michael Fokine, the greatest genius of all choreographers.

And a teacher of ballet, Enrico Cecchetti, with his Latin wizardry in the mimic Art, the *Maître* above all others His was direct descent from Noverre, whom David Garrick, the English actor, had called 'the Shakespeare of the Dance'.

The two dance prodigies of the age danced hand in hand —Anna Pavlova and Vaslav Nijinsky. Yet, while Nijinsky, that astonishing man, could sink his personality sufficiently to blend into the huge canvas that was the Diaghilev Ballet and be part of that design, the dominance and uniqueness of Pavlova's appeal was such that she just could not.

Like Sir Henry Irving, another famous English actor, she

had made herself a bright particular star, and that she always remained. Poor plays were often the fare given by the eminent actor, but he 'made' them, for they were chosen as perfect vessels for his own particular Art. Pavlova's case was, years later, a parallel one. Ready to go into any frame that held Dancing, it was always inevitable she should become the entire picture. With brilliant wisdom for a girl not long reached twenty-one, she realised this Russian Ballet was not her setting, and she left it.

Diaghilev, it is said, never quite forgave her action, nor forgot ; but Anna, searching, had not yet found the true home for her work— as, wisely, she knew. Always she knew what she wanted and acted on it, uninfluenced by others, unlike her confrère in art, Nijinsky, with his easily swayed nature and inability to assess his own talents.

Something—Fate ?—drew her towards London. Pavlova felt that this was where she belonged. But in what way ?

Two milestones had been passed, her debut in Russia and her success in Paris. What was ahead ? Uncertainty and risk assuredly. Many anxious hours to be borne and surmounted. Yet when has the unknown crushed the spirit of an adventurer ? It is his whole life, this thrill of finding out what is just around the next bend in the road.

Surely Pavlova's most ambitious hopes could never have quite visualised all there was : an individual triumph arising from an individual endeavour such as no other dancer has ever known.

From the time of the elf-like Taglioni, the Victorian Ballerina, and before, London has always loved the solo artist. The affection of the largest city in the world has time and again proved warm and steadfast to its favourites, of whatever nationality. For it is perhaps especially a British trait to give love to the one rather more than to be dazzled by the ensemble. Admittedly 'the perfect whole' was the magnet which drew the artists in all genres to the original Diaghilev Ballet Russe, but the general public, the man in the street, likes to have his attention focused on one star. Already for the Russian Ballet there were Nijinsky fans, Pavlova fans, Cecchetti fans, later to include Karsavina fans, followed by a host of others, all vying amongst themselves for the supremacy of their own particular choice. In the entire history of the British Theatre this is noticeable, and not least so in the subsequent adoration of Pavlova, so soon to prove herself a genuine priestess of the Dance, taking it as a torch to illumine the darkest and farthest places of the globe where no Russian Ballet had ever reached.

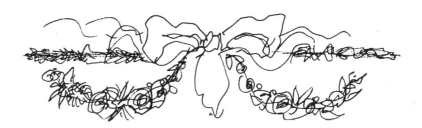

3

'HAVE you seen Pavlova at the Palace Theatre?' everyone was asking.

Pavlova had become a star of the first magnitude overnight.

Her agent, Daniel Mayer, claimed her to be 'The dancing revelation of the age', and that is exactly what she was. Nothing quite like her had ever been seen before. Sir Alfred Butt paid her £160 a week at the start, but soon it was raised to £1,200, and that was a very big salary in those days when a pound meant such a great deal more than it does now.

This, too, was by no means for the entire evening's entertainment. The Opera House, for which this Palace Theatre was originally intended, had for many years been a Music Hall—that is, the programme usually consisted of one star artist at the top of the bill, and lesser-known artists to fill out the time. Therefore the limit allotted to the Russian Dancers was not above forty minutes, possibly less, during which Pavlova herself appeared for say four items—two solo dances and two duets. Yet in that short while, facing the public for about twelve minutes in all at each show, her artistry was so overwhelming that her name immediately became famous literally throughout the world.

The season of Russian Dancers headed by Pavlova, who was partnered by Michael Mordkin and supported by a *corps de ballet* of approximately eight men and women dancers, were the ' rage ' of the London season. Packed houses were a daily occurrence, and the demand, the imperative demand, was ever for more.

Almost at once special Pavlova Matinées were announced for every Wednesday, and at these the Pavlova fans really gave themselves up to it. The pavement of Shaftesbury Avenue was congested with queues for the gallery and the upper circle, seats at 1s and 2s—if one waited long enough ; two hours were usually necessary for getting in, often longer. To stand also : no-one dared leave, for in those days there were no sixpenny stools one could hire to keep a place. Those fortunate people who could afford it, engaged boys to stand as

proxy for them until they arrived about twenty minutes before the doors opened.

Then followed the rush up those seemingly endless stairs to get a seat in the front row. It *was* good to sit down! Sandwiches were unwrapped and eaten in haste, though there was no reason for haste, as the audience had half an hour before curtain up, but all were impatient— impatient for the dancing to begin.

Finally the orchestra struck up with *Marche Russe*, by Ganne, the overture, followed by the parting in the centre of the heavy velvet curtains. Anticipation reached fever-point— but here was only the entrance of two footmen, in livery and powdered wigs, who solemnly marched to each side of the proscenium to affix a card bearing a number. Oh— not Pavlova ! Only the *corps de ballet*, in *Mazurka*, by Glinka. Relax, although with an effort ; but the effective black-and-white Polish costumes and the joyously spirited rhythm were exhilarating, enhanced by a gay sound of tiny bells jingling, produced by a minute cymbal fixed between heel and sole of the dancers'

high white kid boots. There followed one or two other concerted items.

Then Pavlova's number was heralded by a huge crescendo of applause, quickly quietened when it was realised that the solo was *La Nuit*, a beautiful flowing dance in classical dress to Rubinstein's music. Too soon it ended, but the lovely movement was extended by Pavlova's gracious bow—in those cloudy draperies she looked like a hyacinth bending in a gentle breeze. Her dark eyes and dark hair, some thought, resembled the midnight skies, her vibrant spirit the bright star shining through. . . .

There came another wait while the Company performed. Excellent as they were it seemed to the audience rather a waste of time, but naturally Pavlova could not be dancing all the while—apart from anything else, she had to change her dress.

However, presently again two Solos, *Le Cygne* (The Swan) and *Le Papillon* (The Butterfly). What a glorious contrast they were!

'The Dying Swan'—what can there be said about it that is new? Famous writers, the world over, have gone into paeans of praise time and again. Surely no other solo dance has had the publicity that this three minutes of movement started. Was it magic?

Michael Fokine, the undisputed master of the choreographic art, created it specially for Pavlova, suggested, so it is said, by him to the famous ballerina herself when they were watching the elegant grace of a swan in a public park. Certainly no subject could have suited her better, physically, technically and, above all, aesthetically. Anna Pavlova's long slim legs, high-arched insteps and graceful neck, carrying a graciously poised head on sloping shoulders, were ideal for making the onlooker visualise the queenly bird.

Technically she possessed the two essentials, the perfect fifth position 'pointes' run, and a supple yet strong back. Her frail thin arms and eloquent hands expressed most poignantly pain, and the melancholy in her temperament caused the audience to yearn over her ; but through it all there was a grandeur. . . . There is a saying of the momentary rallying of anyone dying that this is a 'swan song'. A swan is reputed to sing during its last moments, the one time in its entire life when it does. Pavlova made one remember this, even in movement only, and so it was glorious as well as

being so very sad. The lights dimmed at last on that still figure. . . .

Tears ran down the faces of many. Then, at last, applause swelling to a thunderous clamour.

People ' came down to earth ' again while Pavlova changed her dress (or did they ?). Now sunshine flooded the stage and suddenly it was a glorious summer's day. ' Papillon '—no pale-blue butterfly this (nothing pallid ever for Pavlova), but a gorgeous golden amber one. Painted wings over a yellow tu-tu, all flashing in the dazzling brightness. It was breath-taking ! Death had gone : here was Life, the Butterfly, living every second of its all too short span, giving all of itself in splendour and colour to enchant all eyes that could see.

This poem of a dance lasted one minute— one minute to impress itself on the beholders for all their lives.

The audience became almost hysterical in their claps and cheers ; then things settled down once more to the usual routine of ensemble dances, revived periodically by a Solo by Mordkin, Pavlova's partner. He was an exceptional dancer, a dominant personality, always interesting to watch— though always second to Pavlova of course : no-one ever managed to equal Pavlova.

Together, they were a wonderful combination, in, among other duets, *Valse Caprice*, a joyous frolic ; but *the* duet always came at the very end— *L'Automne Bacchanale*, to the thrilling music from Glazounov's *Les Saisons*.

To describe a Pavlova night thus in detail is not by any means to convey the impression gained at the time. Thus with *L'Automne Bacchanale*, the thing was not so much a question of what it meant, for really all that it meant was joy at a wine harvest. But what it meant to those who saw it was—joy, joy, joy. . . . All the Golden Age of Greece danced before them, the bas-relief on an antique vase suddenly came to life. Pavlova typified everything feminine, joy, love and tenderness, and Mordkin was the personification of manhood, all-conquering and glorying in his strength. As with any true work of Art, the result was not merely wondrous, but genuinely satisfying, complete—that is why it was chosen as the last dance.

Though not always : many times the audience just would not cease clapping until it had been danced all over again !

Curtain after curtain, one final bow, and then a rush downstairs to be first in the queue at the stage door to watch Pavlova come out.

More standing was rewarded when finally her beloved public saw their favourite gaily smiling, with that engaging expression of friendly sympathy which fitted one's every mood. She held bouquets in her arms, and promptly began to distribute them to her adoring admirers, laughing happily, throwing them from the car ; then she was driven off home. Home—how she must have welcomed its peace and quiet, for these were hectic days for a simple young woman.

It was not long before she took over Ivy House at Golders Green, once the residence of Turner, the painter. Maybe the lovely garden held most appeal— there was even a lake where she could have a swan. Later she had many other birds in a vast aviary.

In those days, just before the First World War, life went along very smoothly and comfortably for the rich in England. Existence for them was less complicated than now. Servants were plentiful and cheap, and ' Society ' entertained in the grand manner, with receptions and balls, inviting hundreds of guests. For these occasions they engaged, at fabulous fees, operatic stars from Covent Garden, and, of course, the great Pavlova herself. Her appearance would not occur until midnight or later, because she had to come on after the Palace Theatre performance.

Victor Dandré, a Russian *avocat* (barrister), was a constant attendant about this time, and later he and Pavlova were married.

4

DURING her season at 'the Palace' it was announced that Pavlova would take a few selected English children as pupils. The anxiety to gain this chance for their own daughters was a united mothers' hope.

First, Madame Pavlova wished to see each child dance.

Scores, maybe hundreds, of mothers and children trudged up the hill from Golders Green station to Ivy House, full of hope.

Daily, each morning, Pavlova patiently endured watching the good, the poor and the bad aspirants.

Finally, amid as much as can be imagined of tears and a little temper from those rejected, Pavlova made her final decision and chose eight.

The dancers did not realise their luck as much as their mothers did. After all it was rather a perilous adventure, and they already felt the impossible would be expected of them— by their parents assuredly, and probably by Pavlova too.

However, terms were settled : sixty guineas for sixty class lessons, to be held four times a week during the Palace Theatre season, the remaining lessons to be taken the following summer. Generous terms, for at that time it was five guineas for one private lesson with Madame.

The classes began.

The eldest child may have been just in her teens, the others were all rather younger. Their names were June (later Lady Inverclyde), Aileen, Beatrice, another Beatrice, Grace, Muriel, Maisie and Helen May.

Madame took each class personally without any assistants except for Walford Hyden, who was at the piano.

French is the language of all Ballet terms and Pavlova spoke mostly in that tongue, for English was very difficult to her then.

The fact that the pupils' French was strictly limited created something of an impasse ; for although the Ballerina showed each step, her pupils' imitation of it was so unlike a replica that often Madame could not believe that the child could have seen what she demonstrated. Soon she learnt to wail distractedly, ' But darling, I nevair show like zat ! ' And of course she never did. . . .

Occasionally Pavlova wore a classical tunic at class, but mostly an everyday dress. As the fashion then was the hobble-skirt this did not improve matters. This skirt, slim and long, was quite absurdly narrow at the hem. Only small steps in walking were possible, so it can be imagined how difficult it was for the dancer to demonstrate or the pupils to see.

Naturally Madame lifted it, but then the arm movements were
lost. Often Pavlova gave up the struggle, sat down and
showed the steps with her hands, a method entirely successful
with advanced pupils but not for these groping beginners,
who must have seemed all feet, without knowing what to do
with them.

Small wonder that she welcomed Phyllis Bedells, the
delightful British dancer who had recently taken over Adeline
Genée's rôles at the Empire Theatre. Madame used to
beseech the children to ' Regarde Philipsa ', which they did in
both the English and French definition of that word.

It was pleasant to recognise much in the Ivy House ball-
room, for in the souvenir programme of the Pavlova season

had been pictures of Cecchetti teaching Pavlova in her St Petersburg studio. A large portrait hangs on the wall; Pavlova is shown in a huge mirror with a trough for growing flowers all along the base of it, and Cecchetti is seated at the piano in the same chair Walford Hyden used at Ivy House. In fact, all here was the same as in that programme, except for a stove in the corner of the Russian studio.

One picture showed the Ballerina doing the ' *Seconde pliez portes de bras*', the *Maître* indicating with his little cane, as he always did. From time to time, whenever possible Pavlova took lessons from him, for years after this.

Darlings both—small wonder they were such kindred spirits ! One of the pupils is eternally grateful that two such busy folk should have visited those pupils' performances.

Frequently when the class was over, dozens of children and grown-ups would be waiting to dance to Pavlova. The pupils and mothers used to crowd at the *portière* to the large ballroom and watch. Some were terribly bad, some almost funny, if one had felt unkind. Now and again when a child was good Madame would praise her ; but later, reading in London newspapers, ' Child dancer highly admired by the Great Ballerina ', she was furious and declared, ' Now I say nozzing ! ' She had not praised to give the child publicity.

There were those who danced the ' Swan ' to her. When unbearable, Madame would murmur, ' Thank you,' and if this had no result, ' *C'est assez.*'

Then if even this outspokenness did not suffice, a cold hard voice would say, ' Go home ! '

A great man once maintained that ' the true art of memory is attention '. This proved true enough with the pupils : those who progressed most were the children who looked and listened most. Madame herself used to ask after a step was danced correctly, ' *Mais oui, ma chérie*, but can you take it 'ome wiz you, or is it only in your eyes ? ' For some could only do it as though it were a copy of a photograph, then forget it afterwards.

With the charming thought of pleasing them, Pavlova decided that her ' babies ', as she called them, should dance at her own garden-party on the lawn by the lake.

That was indeed a treat for them, as was a repeat performance at a huge political garden-party where ten thousand guests attended, headed by Bonar Law, later to be Prime Minister, in what had once been Horace Walpole's house at Strawberry Hill.

34

Better still was the news, in August 1912, of a special pupils' Matinée at the Palace Theatre.

In a miniature ballet of Pavlova's own devising, called *La Naissance de Papillon* (The Birth of a Butterfly), they represented various wild flowers, Pavlova herself the butterfly. It was indeed a thrill to be wearing a real ballet skirt for the first time !

Rehearsals were held on Sundays and the children enjoyed many happy afternoons roaming freely in the house and garden, becoming acquainted with her pets, trying to make friends with Jack the swan, who, however, remained aloof and coldly indifferent on his lake except when Madame came. He knew her and would coil his long neck about her in a most affectionate way.

As ever, Pavlova gave love abundantly and received it in return. She truly loved her eight little pupils and they adored her—for herself alone, not just as their dancing divinity.

If only they could just once dance a little like her. . . . But ' if wishes were horses, beggars would ride '. Youthful ambitions that appeared impossible to attain were much soothed, however, by the generous Russian teas that followed rehearsals, and young appetites made short work of the rich cakes, regardless of all the fat-creating cream. Pavlova laughed to see their joy, and the parrot screeched his raucous approval !

The mothers had their share of attention too, for Madame was a most gracious hostess with a great regard for parents. Recently her own little mother had come over from Russia to enjoy with her daughter the latter's triumph. Roaming about the garden with her arm about the other's shoulders, Pavlova was both tender and proud.

How far that clever daughter had gone since those humble days in the Russian countryside ! Many miles indeed—yet she remained the same, unspoilt and fond. Still true to her old love of Nature, too, as her solos symbolised, for they mostly portrayed a bird, an insect or a flower. ' Art is Nature seen through a temperament '—thus were Pavlova's Solo Dances.

The longed-for and yet dreaded day of the Pupils' Matinée drew near. Madame's care for her ' babies ' was such that she darned their ballet shoes. Fearing they might slip, possibly fall, this being in most instances their first appearance on any stage, she took their slippers with her in the car and criss-crossed the tips of the toes while she was travelling to and from the Palace Theatre. Who but she would have taken so much trouble ? Who but she would have managed to take it, sewing such neat small stitches while in a moving car ?

Nothing was ever too much trouble for her. One pupil's most vivid recollection of that entire performance was seeing Pavlova, just before the children were to make their entrance, on her knees in the wings anxiously stitching a last-minute repair to one of the dresses.

Halcyon Days, over all too soon ; for presently Pavlova was away on a tour, and her pupils had to wait for more lessons until their lovely bird flew home again.

Another whole year—a lifetime, it seemed, at eleven—before classes would be resumed.

Finally the time did arrive, but after yet one more glorious season of lessons and Pavlova Matinées, on a bright summer morning in August 1914, war was declared. In a sudden stroke, life was no longer the same for anybody. From a carefree existence everyone turned to being serious ; and the taken-for-granted security that child-hood then enjoyed went, of course, with everything else. It was all very terrifying and quite incomprehensible to the young.

5

THE war upset everything. Air-raids, Zeppelins over London
— moonlight no longer reminded one of Pavlova's *La Nuit*, but
only brought the horror of bombs.

Amid all the panic and the sorrow, Pavlova still danced,
her tireless feet carrying her around the world to give comfort
to millions. What a worthy mission, and how nobly performed ! The Dance must go on, and so it did—with Pavlova.
Pointing the way to all those truly devoted to it, she showed

in her personal integrity what it meant to say that one had a vocation.

In charity she gave a practical and very real assistance : no need, whether personal or public, was ever ignored. The tragic earthquake in Japan — Pavlova gave a special performance to raise funds for the homeless. And children everywhere were a never-failing appeal.

What she lost in having no children of her own she made up for by helping others, founding and maintaining a Home for poor mites in Paris, among many other generous grants, too numerous to mention, but each a proof of her all-embracing love. For love had always been the secret of her success. Members of an audience felt that she was dancing to each one individually, because to each she conveyed just that message of love.

' Publica ! ' she used to cry to her pupils who oft-times danced with downcast eyes. ' Regarde la publique ! ' In other words, give all you have of worth, as she did of her heaven-endowed talent. Never did her dancing appear to say ' Look at me ; am I not wonderful ! ' but ever ' Join in with me ; isn't dancing wonderful ! '

Generosity was there, too, overflowing generosity that was part of love, the true artist's desire to share with everyone the beautiful experience in the realms of beauty that the artist himself enjoys.

In a world of shifting values, of complete instability, Pavlova retained balance. Her motto might have been that of the first Queen Elizabeth, ' Always the same '.

Although she had travelled over the entire globe, meeting her again at Ivy House one could not realise how far she had been since the last meeting. Seeing her calm serenity was alone an inspiration ; there seemed no need to travel to see the wonders of the world, for as a Tudor poet wrote, she made ' one little room an everywhere '.

As a sympathetic listener she shone. ' Anything you fear is wrong,' she used to say. How right that idea was, and as usual Pavlova lived her truths.

Fearlessly she continued her own course, to take dancing to all peoples. Sailing over the oceans threatened danger from submarines. Dauntlessly Pavlova travelled. Regardless of peril she was the courier of the Dance. While there were yet places, some maybe tucked away in the far corners of the earth, however small, who knew not the ballet, she must show it to them. Show them not Pavlova, mind you, but Dancing.

Dancing was her job, and she did it always to the best of her ability. At many places slackness of performance would never have been noticed, for they had no standards of comparison, but Pavlova had ! It was *she* whom she must satisfy. Only perfection could do that.

This was Pavlova's war work, to give love, joy, life, truth and beauty—the positive qualities—to a world surfeited with the negatives, hate, sorrow, death, falsehood and ugliness.

Needing a courageous spirit to brave the dangers and bear the hardships, it was miraculous how these tours were achieved. Mr Dandré coped with all the anxiety of running a big company, and no doubt, in his kindly way, he helped his wife in every detail that was possible ; but it was Pavlova who had to dance.

Long, long train journeys, cramped with fatigue ; then the theatre, practice, rehearsals, shows. All this to be done, not by a bold brassy star, brandishing her importance, but by a sensitive woman with the highly strung nature of the Artist combined with the conscientiousness of the ' Religieuse '.

An impression may be gained from all this zeal that Pavlova must have been forbiddingly tense. Not so. Frivolous moments abounded. Work was work, play was play. As with Shakespeare's Cleopatra, one of her greatest charms was that custom could not stale her infinite variety. In party mood her spirit of mischief was captivating, like that of a child full of fun. And her mimicry !— this was superb. To watch Pavlova ' taking off ' any amusing incident was unique.

Small wonder that she and Charles Chaplin found so much of mutual interest when they met in California. There was a photograph of this in the London Museum at the Pavlova Exhibition, with the same urchin expression on both their faces, as though mud-pie days were not long, if at all, forgotten.

London never forgot her either, although seasons were infrequent during those difficult days.

The War lasted over four years ; then came Armistice Day, which we still honour each November.

With the ceasing of hostilities London put on a gay face. Lights went up again, and people believed that it had been a war to end war. Little did they know that twenty years later there would be a second, lasting even longer. . . .

43

The world seemed to go completely mad with joy in hysterical reaction to all that it had been through. Of ball-room dancing, the kindest thing that could be said was that it showed almost the lowest depth to which Dancing can sink. But Pavlova still retained the highest standard, her own, and it was, once again, a revelation to watch her.

The theatre world, freed from nights of blackout, flourished once more, and what more enchanting vision of a new Spring could there be than Pavlova? Ever young, ever fresh, and now more frequently appearing—and wholly gladdening the life of one of her former pupils by the presentation of a stage

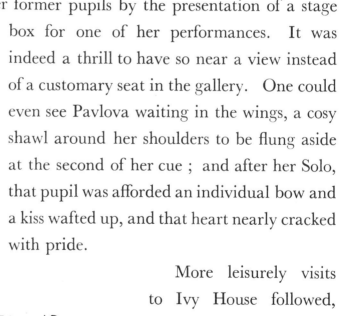

box for one of her performances. It was indeed a thrill to have so near a view instead of a customary seat in the gallery. One could even see Pavlova waiting in the wings, a cosy shawl around her shoulders to be flung aside at the second of her cue ; and after her Solo, that pupil was afforded an individual bow and a kiss wafted up, and that heart nearly cracked with pride.

More leisurely visits to Ivy House followed, with intimate chats and much long-delayed news to exchange.

Madame was really

interested in English dancers and wished to know all about any new ones. When assured that she herself spoilt us for all the others, she smiled deprecatingly. All the same, her face lit up. It might have been the first compliment she had ever received, she who had been fêted by all, kings

and gallery girls alike. She was alluringly natural as of old. Achievement and praise were merely work and its reward. After striving greatly, her prize had been great. That was but justice.

No personal conceit marred Pavlova's outlook, for that would have been falsehood, which she detested. Like Caesar conquering the world, one triumph was but a spur to further endeavour. And so triumph had succeeded triumph, a long procession throughout the years, and she was happy with her heart's content.

Having known the other side of the coin, poverty and struggle, she was like *Hamlet's* Horatio, ' in suffering all, that suffers nothing ', one who ' fortune's buffets and rewards had ta'en with equal thanks '.

This serenity does not tally with what has been said of a bad temper. Or does it? When the sea is calm, sunlight shimmering on the surface, there is yet a tempest beneath ready to yield to the power of the wind and be lashed to fury.

So with Pavlova, for being very human her faults were human. Stupidity did enrage her : caused too often by laziness, it was not to be borne. She did not suffer in silence any more than she kept happiness to herself. Her articulate nature would have made both impossible.

Patient she was, wonderfully so, with the pupils. Her sense of justice admitted that they were very young and could not be expected to know everything.

Tolerant she was not. Grown girls in her Company complained of this and possibly truthfully. Still, there were very likely faults on both sides. It was a clash of women all strained to breaking-point, often exhausted with the fatigue of travel and work.

Admittedly, Pavlova was a martinet, none stricter. Saving herself never entered her calculations, so why should she save others? Justice is a hard master with no leniency to frail humanity. The famous dancer was no different from Napoleon and other great leaders.

Genius exacts penalties from those it favours. Soaring continuously, the climber gazes inevitably to the heights, and in so doing loses interest with much that has been left behind. If the laggards cannot follow they must be ignored. A hard law but a just one, for genius is rare indeed, the others legion. Walking alone, genius does tend to foster selfishness as a protection from a harsh world.

How were these hard-worked dancers to fathom the complexity of Pavlova? Impossible! It is necessary to be impartial to see both sides of any dispute. Fact, not prejudice, must be faced, and there was no time for that. The tour, like a juggernaut, rolled on, crushing their strength and numbing their ability to think with its inexorable demands. 'The gentle art of dancing'—who wrote that? Obviously whoever it was did not realise the strenuous labour that must be undergone to make it appear *just that*.

The Company saw the world, however, although fatigue often made them unable to appreciate fully all its wonders, all its treasures. Many travellers return from far lands no richer for their experience. Knowledge is gained not by what is seen by the eye but what is felt in the soul.

Primarily these girls had to earn their living. Not only did they work very hard, they were exceptionally good dancers,

and everywhere, save in the proximity of Pavlova, they would have been seen to be of star quality. Nothing could compete with Pavlova, however. Thus their life was a job merely, often tedious and full of drudgery. Little wonder if they lost interest in themselves at times. Pavlova never did ; at work or play her eye was on them.

Romance stirs the dancer as it stirs everyone else, and then she was the most understanding companion. Once a member

48

of the Company was having her honeymoon in the south of France. Pavlova heard and took the happy couple about in her car, even accompanying them on a charabanc trip. In a Paris dress of flaming chiffon and a large picture-hat, the Ballerina laughed gaily and munched a banana. . . . Later she confided, ' You wise girl. He good man.'

Apparently, like Napoleon, Pavlova needed little sleep, for often on dreary train journeys in America she would sit in her girls' bunks, and during the long night entertain them with stories of the St Petersburg School.

Beauty thrilled her always, India and its treasures—but it was her soul that they stirred. She told the girls, ' Yes, you see Taj Mahal by moonlight. All romance for you, you young, but not for me ! '

Never appearing to realise her own wonderful youth and skill, she always noted it in others, making one former pupil very happy by a personal letter of appreciation of her work as a teacher.

When was she not giving ?

Her pupils treasured all : boxes of chocolates, or a work box, for sewing, at Christmas (she even learnt each child's favourite colour), an album containing photographs of her

and those same pupils, or a large picture of herself, again inscribed individually, and signed 'With love from Anna Pavlova'. Even a pair of her ballet shoes when a pupil had forgotten to bring her own to class.

Her own dancing corsets, too, on one occasion. It may sound untrue— Pavlova, with her freedom, dancing in corsets ? But she explained that years ago the students at the Russian School had worn them when dancing with a partner, saying, ' Then when he lift you, thumbs do not press so much, and you do not get appendicitis.' (She did *not* mention that in this case it was a utility gift, with the hope that the corset might give the plump child some kind of a figure.)

During her tours, Pavlova was not long in acquiring a knowledge of the National Dances of many lands, and eventually audiences saw presentations of Spanish, Mexican and Indian dances, as well as those of other countries, including Japan.

Anything in which she danced was interesting, but the majority of her audience preferred her as a ballerina. Other lesser dancers could have given them these studies. It seemed a waste of Pavlova. Everyone wanted her in a tu-tu, for that was her natural element.

(A bouquet should be handed here to Manya, who made these exquisite creations. Her ballet dresses were masterpieces, not only the frothy frills which danced with Pavlova but the imagination and variety employed in the bodices, too often dully drab and uninteresting or else glaringly showy with a deal of cheap glitter.)

To many people no nylon innovations, or fish-net hose, have managed successfully to supersede the elegant sheen of pure silk tights—which were what Pavlova always wore.

Her ballet skirts were varied in style. From the long tarlatan frills in *Christmas*, with the delightful pink taffeta coat, bonnet and muff, trimmed with swansdown in the authentic Victorian fashion, to *The Swan*, with a short skirt of swan feathers. A gold and crimson dress was memorable in the first Palace Theatre days for a *pas de deux* with Mordkin. *Fairy Doll* also had a short skirt, in a gay pink, and gossamer puffed sleeves— not forgetting the Wand.

Accessories such as wands, cymbals, scarves and the like, when carried by some tend to appear merely as aids to give the arms something to do. With Pavlova they accented the character. Such was her aptness that one felt no scarf or fan had been handled with such grace and charm before.

All her costumes were poems when she wore them, the tu-tu and the others. The sumptuous long jewel-encrusted robe for a *Grand Russe* duet, with the high 'Troika' head-dress. Very original, 'Californian Poppy', with its wired golden petals to simulate the flower. Another wired ingenuity was 'Dragonfly', with long slim iridescent wings. It must be realised that Pavlova was not only skilful with a fan : she could take on the manipulation of an intricate dress. With what infinite charm she folded herself up in the petals of the Poppy as the light dimmed to indicate the approach of night! And as a Dragonfly, slim arms curved along the gossamer

wings and one saw the flight of the scintillating insect. Nature, life itself— that was the inspiration. Every simple object in her eloquent hands was enhanced in beauty.

A sword in the duet with Laurent Novikoff, from the Ballet *Don Quixote*, became an ideal complement to her long slim legs. Noted for her unsurpassed arabesque, in this adage movement the tip of the rapier on the ground seemed no weightier nor more slender than the ' pointe ' of her foot.

Amarilla, that ballet never forgotten for the Gipsy Girl's duet with her ' brother ' (Novikoff, a splendid mime combining the look and physique of a Greek god with the musical sensitivity of the real Artist, was an ideal partner)— the tawny draperies conveyed an effect of poverty and a raggle-taggle existence.

Flowing gowns for *La Nuit*, *Valse Caprice*, *Giselle* (second act) accentuated the melody of Pavlova's every movement, each line— or rather, curve— melting into the next.

None could forget *Gavotte Pavlova*, with an Empire-period yellow satin gown, high waisted, worn with a matching poke-bonnet, from which streamed long ribbons.

The tu-tu with a Spanish flavour for *Paquita*, in black and gold. But every design was arresting in its way, nothing insipid was ever worn by Madame. As she said to her small pupils, ' I do not want your pretty feet, your pretty faces—I want Caractère.' This quality abounded in her clothes, both stage and private, as it abounded in her dancing.

Arresting ever—cloying never. Not for Pavlova the antics of a simpering miss, meaningless and artificial.

As with Nijinsky, who said the word 'graceful' made him feel sea-sick, for it was so inadequate, so would Pavlova have loathed the description 'dainty'. Futile descriptions, for to dance well it is obvious one *must* be both. Graceful and dainty, of course, but more—oh! much, much more!

Choreography, like all else, was taken in her stride, and her poignant ballet *Autumn Leaves*, to the melodies of Chopin, was a beautiful piece of work, with Pavlova as a Chrysanthemum in a most endearing dress of shaded chiffon with trailing flower petals. It was not unlike an early Solo, *La Rose qui Meurt*. Pavlova, as fragile as a petal, melted one's heart in tender compassion for this whiff of perfume that was dying.

Dying . . .?

Little did a certain pupil think about death when, that Christmas, she was invited for tea at Ivy House at five o'clock. Madame had heard it called ' five o'clock tea ' in England, so, being of a literal mind, at five o'clock tea always was for her. She rested when she could in the afternoon, but punctual to the tick, were she at home, at five o'clock she poured tea.

On this day, rapidly cry-ing, ' Quick, Victor, finish —we see Mai dance ' (as though that could be a treat for her—for *I* was Mai !), always ready for a party, Pavlova clapped, laughingly demanding from me all the most difficult steps she could think of.

A small gift I had brought of home-made

toffees was shared with Pierre Vladimiroff, her last partner, and her husband, and with a little furrier who was busy in a corner of the studio, selecting sables to make Madame a fur coat. None dreamed she would not live to wear it. . . .

All seemed normal in its delightfully unusual way. The hostess was as ever interested in everything. No possible hint of that dark tragedian, Death, already waiting in the wings for his cue. In the hall, as of old on the eve of departure, were the two enormous trunks.

She kissed me good-bye at the front door just as usual, and there appeared no warning shadow—until :

The evening paper of 23 January 1931 announced in huge type at the top of the front page :

DEATH OF PAVLOVA

It seemed unbelievable ! But one read on, and the tragic details were revealed. While travelling to the Hague there had been an accident to the train—nothing very serious, but it had meant standing about on the track in the cold. When Madame and the Company reached Paris after the delay, her first thought, as ever, was to practise. The studio, however, was not heated adequately.

Undaunted, Pavlova did practise, but by the time the Hague was reached it was obvious that she had a chill. A doctor insisted that she go to bed and stay there. Pavlova made nothing of it, and when her husband arrived laughed with him at the absurdity of her being in bed when she felt well.

A fever soon set in, and rapidly turned to pneumonia. 'Poor Pavvie'—as we admirers affectionately named her—this was something even she could not cope with. Other specialists were called in, every remedy tried, but to no avail. She, who was never ill, in three days, like one of her beloved flowers, wilted and died.

During the night of 22 January 1931 she spoke once again, although unconscious for many hours previously. It was her Swan Song. . . .

She asked for her Swan ballet dress. Subconsciously her mind was on her work—her last thought was of dancing. . . . So died the Ballet's greatest exponent.

No dancer has ever been so widely known. Even those who never saw her, who were born long after her death, say, 'Oh, yes ! I've heard of Pavlova.'

The evening paper's heading had been DEATH OF PAVLOVA—no more. There was no mention of who she was, for there was no need—the whole world knew.

After the shock of reading the news had abated a little, one thought what a pity it was that she should die so young and while still dancing beautifully.

Yet—was it ?

As with Nelson, it was fitting that she should go with her medals shining upon her.

She was a perfectionist, and it would have been heart-breaking to see her powers gradually diminish and be unable to prevent it. More heartbreaking for her. . . .

Much better this way, to die in a blaze of glory, as the sun sets.

Funerals are harrowing at all times, and Pavlova, the joyous one, would wish to be remembered as dancing, or at least amid her flowers. So it is not unhappy to think of her in death at that colourful lying-in-state at the Russian church.

For two whole days her admirers from all parts of the world walked slowly past the richly draped coffin to pay their last respects to the greatest ballerina of all. The ballerina who had delighted them on so many countless occasions, but who now would dance no more. The Swan would not flutter her wings again. Giselle would no longer leap through the woods.

Many friends placed bouquets at her feet—how many times had they not done that before?—while the choir filled the beautiful church with song. And there we leave the little Pavlova, in the midst of a mound of flowers.

Was there a whisper of voice asking in mild surprise, 'All zis for *me*?'

6

Anna Pavlova is dead, but the Dying Swan is immortal !

It is Auction Day at Ivy House. Newspapers might say that the Swan had died, but here on the lake at Ivy House a swan is still gliding gracefully, glistening in its proud beauty, white and gallant, as unruffled as the mirrored surface through which it speeds ; for here is sunshine and it is June.

Out here there is peace, and a sense of ' all's well '. Inside the house all is different : empty rooms, locked and full of memories—memories of rooms crowded with people and furniture. Memories of the Music Room, where she, the one-time Mistress of all this, practised and improved that Art which everyone except herself felt needed no improvement—her music room, now a place of auction, where all her belongings, from the grand piano to her own little manicure set, are going to the highest bidder.

The big mirror, in which as children we pupils learned to notice our mistakes—the many faces once reflected there, would mystify the auctioneer.

There is a thick carpet on the floor : it dulls the scraping of chairs and the fidgeting of feet—yet, clearer than all the muffled sounds, some of us seem to hear her step, light and elegant, that walk that in each movement said with conscious pride for all the world to know, ' I am a dancer '.

Everyone is very polite and quiet, the auctioneer himself magnificently restrained ; but women, tense though subdued, are seated lining the long sides of a large green-baize covered table, their eyes alert, their jewelled fingers restless.

The sun pours down heavily on the glass roof, and one realises that this is a kind of bazaar.

Let us escape to the balcony, silently making our way out. There is only this staircase, red-carpeted and well worn by those little active feet of hers.

Here is friendliness, something remaining as it was ?—no,
a notice obtrudes :

NO SMOKING PERMITTED

and once again one realises that this charming gracious home
is now a public place.

The sale seems unreal when viewed from the balcony,
and one feels nearer in spirit to the darling mistress of the
house.

There is the door of her bedroom, where the pupils used
to watch the breakfast tray go in when waiting for their lesson.
Anon a gaily smiling figure would emerge and flit along to her
bath. Today, Auction Day, an idly curious woman is trying
that door, but the lock won't give ; the lock at least is

true to its absent occupant, and the woman saunters away, nonchalantly chagrined.

Along the corridor a man and woman, no longer young, stand a little apart from the rest and lean over the rail. They have the worn but interesting faces of those who have been for years the fond disciples of an exacting Art. Maybe they were dancers in her Company years ago. They look expectant, in a bewildered kind of way, as though they know not for what they wait, but in their eyes is the pain of memory. . . . Let us escape to the garden.

The front door stands wide, and there on the stone floor where last one kissed her hands in farewell, there stands a policeman, mute epitome of the law of change.

Summer beckons, and we move out into its warmth, trying

not to see the two great trunks standing side by side in the hall, with their large initials A.P. and V.D.—Anna Pavlova and Victor Dandré. For many years these names had stood together thus, together now, two trunks in the hall, packed and waiting to be sent to some place. . . . Can all the really individual belongings of two personalities be contained in so small a space? Two lives in a trunk. . . .

But the world is still green and clear. There is the lawn on which the pupils danced—but even here Summer and Life itself is for sale, for there are labels on all the flower-pots.

The aviary is silent and empty, no feathered song to cheer the stillness. All tense and stopped, like death itself. . . .

Only the swan on the lake glides on and on, round and round in its little pool of light, as though it defied death. . . .

Proud it always was, proud in its beauty, yet now it has more reason for pride, for has not its beloved Mistress immortalised its name *Le Cygne*—'The Dying Swan'? Dying, maybe, yet never dead.

Anna Pavlova's body is dead, but her Swan will live for ever. It is right in defying death.

There was a Memorial Performance, presented by Mr Dandré, at which it was evident that the Swan *would* live for ever.

In the darkened theatre the entire audience stood in

homage while the orchestra began the opening bars of that haunting music.

The curtain rose on the dimly lit stage, one little pool of white light moving slowly in the path her feet would have glided. Everyone had seen them dozens of times. It seemed that they could see them still. Any moment now, one felt, surely Pavlova would be dancing with her girls?

As the last notes died away a unanimous sigh broke the stillness, the curtain slowly fell. Its gentle swish accompanied a great sob from that vast audience.

One awoke unwillingly, and tried to take an interest in reality, the reality of the ballet that followed.

Inspired, the girls danced as never before, and without the inevitable comparison with Pavlova it was apparent what really excellent dancers they were.

Yet another performance, given by the Camargo Society, honoured the memory of Pavlova in the same manner. The Swan *was* immortal. That beautiful bird had been immortalised for all time by the little dancer from Russia.

And it still glided on the lake at Ivy House, and the ivy, a further everlasting reminder, still grew there. Not far away a beautiful white marble urn rested in a niche on a wall, with flowers about it (some tall lilies like those Pavlova herself would bring back from Covent Garden market early on a

summer morning). Within it lay her ashes. . . .

Her ashes— she had wished to be cremated—are scattered in Golders Green, in the Garden of Remembrance, that happy perfumed place of peace and liberation, of growing trees that, too, dance, dance in the breeze, trees that give shade and shelter to the birds, and flowers everywhere.

' East Wall 3211 ' no longer means anything but a necessary identification in a book of record of cremations.

Pavlova, the real Pavlova, has escaped—to dance to her heart's content. . . .

No distance away there is another garden, that retreat she loved, the garden of Ivy House, where, in Ivy Cottage, Paul Smikitis, her Russian gardener, still lives, a vital personality dreaming of all the flowers he tended for his beloved Mistress. Fun glints from his intelligent eyes and one can tell that Madame would have thought a lot of him still, a face full of the enjoyment of every living minute even at eighty-seven.

It was a typical gesture that she should give him that home for all his life.

Today the rest of her home is a hospital, a place of healing.

68

That is fitting, also. It was always an abode of comfort, with Pavlova herself tending her 'babies'.

Whenever one is wearying for a sight of Pavlova, it is very rewarding to visit Ivy Cottage. As in an 'Indian Summer' the sunshine returns once more, and not even a very wet day can damp the fire of Paul's recollections.

On the afternoon of his birthday every year Madame came to tea. Smiling, he remarks, 'Lovely cake I have, rich, give big piece to Madame, but always she-not eat, just cut off leetle slice for self and say, " I wish I could eat all, but only permitted so, or I will become fat." We laugh then. Oh, much laughter. She love party, with Pavlova always a party. She have parties all time.'

Continuing, 'When Pavlova have " temperament ", she come to us very angry, staff afraid, they go, run away, I not afraid, I stay. She ask, " Why you not go ? " " Why should I ? " I say. " So ! " she say. . . . Then no more.' Doubtless Pavlova respected him for standing up to her.

Paul Smikitis was in a position of trust with Mr and Mrs Dandré (how odd that looks, although of course it was her name), and when on a tour it was to him they wrote to give addresses of where and when to forward mail—instructions about Ivy House, also when they would be arriving and what to have ready.

69

He had first seen Pavlova dance in Czarist St Petersburg, and coming to London after the Revolution sought out Madame —and was employed as her gardener for the rest of her life.

Showing photographs of her and trying to explain, words often fail him. Mime helps, however, and he will briefly add, ' Pavlova pleased ', ' Pavlova displeased '.

With a twinkle in his eyes, Paul says, ' Madame Pavlova had big temperament, but then I think all nice ladies have big temperament.'

Presently he will interrupt the reminiscences with, ' Excuse please, it is the time. I go cover frame.' He is ever the gardener first, his plants his foremost thought, and Pavlova would appreciate that.

Anything associated with Madame has his protection. In October 1946 a terrific gale played havoc with her favourite mulberry tree. Two-thirds of it was blown down, but the remaining part, skilfully strutted and tended by Paul, should grow to some of its former glory. Pavlova would often sit beneath it, reading or having tea surrounded by her bird friends. She made a lovely picture so, but too soon the central figure would have to step from her frame and become part of a larger canvas, with another world tour and Pavlova painting pictures in the hearts of thousands. All the same, sometimes Ivy House must have been very difficult to leave.

And the birds in her aviary—what became of them, when she no longer returned ? Many of them were given homes by

Pavlova's friends. Still a few remained, and Paul tells how he 'put them in boxes and took—oh! many little boxes—and give here, and here, to more friends.'

Close to Ivy Cottage is the garage. In the old days when the gates were opened one noticed, not strangely the car, but the store of ballet shoes in every conceivable colour stacked high all up one wall. It mattered little if room were left for the car or if it had to be put elsewhere, but the ballet shoes must be housed. That was so like Pavlova's whole life : no stress on luxurious ease, but always a constant attention to work. 'Pavlova always working at something,' Paul affirms.

On one occasion the visitor saw the fireplace strewn with water-colour plans. 'They dry, have got wet,' Paul explained ; then, uncurling the large sheets, 'It is all places where Madame Pavlova lived. See every tree and plant listed, all the flowers. . . . She very happy when she see this, what I make for her.' And well she might have been, for the loving care that had gone into it, made for no reason other than the pleasure of the artist.

He knew her so much as a simple companion, a fellow Russian, that one can sense how her extraordinary fame is still a wonder to him. He is anxious, though, that others shall fully realise its greatness, and he proudly gives proof :

'Soon after Madame die, one day child come to Ivy House, five year, maybe six year old, she must dance in ballroom to say she have where Pavlova danced. So in minute she make

ready, shoes, dress, all on. Her mother play. She dance.
So happy. They go. Ten year later, come again. Knock on
door. I open. " You remember me ? " she ask. A pretty
girl, but why should I remember ? Then she tell, after
ten year, she come see me. So glad she have dance where
Pavlova dance.'

There is a new photograph today on the mantelpiece :
Ulanova down by the lake ; in the background the statue of
Pavlova dancing. The Soviet Ballerina, her nearest possible
successor, made the pilgrimage to the home of her country-
woman.

Another living link is Manya, Pavlova's personal maid.
When asked her name, she always replies, ' Oh, it comes by
the yard—just call me Manya.'

One remembers, before a pupils' matinée, noticing her for
the first time. All she could say in English then was ' Needle
and cotton '. How well she too served Madame.

She and Paul supplied two of the chief needs in Pavlova's
life. She the needle and cotton for Pavlova's work, he the
growing things for her play. How could Pavlova have sur-
vived without Nature and the Dance ?

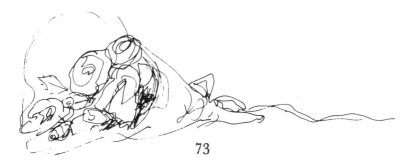

7

I⊤ is a rainy afternoon and, arriving much before the time arranged, a wet visitor waits in the entrance hall of Ivy House. There are hospital sounds in the background, not loud enough to drown the memory of a certain small voice heard for the last time : ' Good-bye, darling, you be good girl and practise, I come again soon. . . .'

Thence across that mosaic paving where her feet had trod, and over the carriage drive to the cottage where the owner never tires of speaking about her.

And so to a chat with Paul, whose memory is excellent, only pausing once to hear Football Results on the wireless—and while this is going on the guest waits quite happily, for is she not seated on a little stool that Pavlova used when she gave her lessons ? It is a bit drab now, painted brown. She remembers it a gleaming white like all the paint in the ball-room. Never mind—that chair came all the way from Madame's St Petersburg studio, and was sat in by Cecchetti at the piano when he taught Pavlova. . . .

Sometimes the housekeeper is present, the third member of those last links with Pavlova. Still vastly efficient, with a fine alert brain, she also paints word pictures of the

happy home life that existed at Ivy House. An English woman, kindly and sympathetic, she completes the living trio of domestic friends who helped so greatly to make the dancer's strenuous life easier. One realises once again that Pavlova not only had a genius for choosing exceptional people, but the rarer ability of retaining their love. Despite the alleged ' temperament ' she was undoubtedly a good mistress, considerate, and in return considered.

Talk turns to Madame's pets. Her dogs. . . . First at Ivy House, a big British bulldog, who had a partiality for ballet skirts — that is, when Madame had discarded one after practice and let it slip to the floor while she rested in a wrapper, he would lie on it at her feet.

Later there was a Pekinese, who often sat on Pavlova's lap during the class ; later still, a French bulldog.

Cats, too, the most noticeable being a Siamese cat who appears in a beautiful picture with Madame, taken on the window seat in the library. That window seat where the little pupils used to change into dance tunics —with what trepidation !

Or Pavlova's bedroom— one recalls changing there one afternoon and stroking

76

the lovely fur of the chinchilla bedspread. Surprise — it was warm, it moved, it *purred*! With a tiny 'miaow' a wee kitten crept over it, shaking its Persian coat.

In the drawing-room Madame had hung the pupils' gift after *The Birth of a Butterfly*. Originally the mothers had got together and had a beautiful yellow satin cushion made, with the wildflowers that the children had represented hand painted on it. For the car, it was suggested, but Madame valued it too greatly and had it framed in gilt. Little did one pupil dream when she wrote her name under the buttercup that she would eventually buy it back in the public auction at Ivy House.

Memories everywhere at Ivy House. . . .

That little room where Pavlova worked at her modelling, those delightful little figurines of herself dancing. How accurately she portrayed each characteristic of movement and form!

Or here, watching Pavlova at her 'side-practice'. Her 'exercices à la barre' were like intricate jewellery, exquisite in every minor detail, smooth and plastic, yet with a sharpness of a first-water diamond. A dance pattern wrought in filigree. . . .

In broad contrast, Pavlova performing a man's solo, bursting with 'ballon' and 'brio'. For it was a very warm Sunday afternoon, too hot for work, her partner said—even the bees were drowsy. Not so Pavlova! At rehearsal one *danced*, so Pavlova danced, the male solo from *La Fille mal Gardée* in a pink-and-white ballet dress.

Pavlova's garden-party—where has the long swinging seat gone that the children sat on while revelling in strawberry ices? At that instant Pavlova herself was a vibrant splash of orange draperies on the green lawn, dancing a duet with Novikoff. At the end one child rushed to hand Madame a huge bouquet of tall lilies tied with a big bow, pink (her favourite colour). The shade was not 'friendly' with the orange, but like a flash Pavlova hid the offending ribbon in the folds of her dress while embracing the little pupil. Always the saver of situations with her quick intuition. . . .

Or the time one of the pupils had stage fright, having to lead in for the *Blue Danube* dance. All suddenly went blank! 'A'right, darling?' anxiously from Pavlova. 'Oui, Madame.' Better to perish than admit one could not remember any of it ! There came the opening bars and with blanched cheeks one entered—and the step was remembered, just in time. . . .

The Palace Theatre, of course, seems almost bursting with memories !

Most thrilling of all is the scenery-dock, that door at the extreme back of the stage where Pavlova and her partner waited for the opening bars of *L'Automne Bacchanale*, beginning the dance there so that speed should be gained when they reached the footlights.

Three minutes later and that tumultuous duet was over, Pavlova full length on the ground in the final pose, only to be up again with the quickness and lightness of a leaf when Novikoff grasped her hand for their bow.

Thunders of applause ! Novikoff finally mounted the stairs to his dressing-room, leaving the curtain calls to Madame. 'Bravo !' shouted again and again by hoarse throats, until Pavlova, streaming with perspiration so that her eye make-up was way down her cheeks, had to rush up those stone stairs, calling, 'Laurent—come ! Publica ! Encore !' And, completely breathless, they danced it all again !

The auditorium, with the mirrors all around the stalls area. It is a Pupils' Matinée—what a thrill to see oneself reflected, dancing on a great London stage !

Or Pavlova's own dressing-room during that same Pupils' Matinée, when a tearful little girl was consoled on Madame's lap and coaxed with chocolates to believe it was ' a'right after all '.

For there had been a hectic last-minute rehearsal for *The Birth of a Butterfly* on stage just before curtain-up. Two scarves had to be removed to reveal Madame as a butterfly. This cocoon idea had not been tried before with the actual scarves, but the dancer was wearing a silk day frock and two pupils took the first, followed by two others for the second, quite easily.

It was another matter at the performance ! The butterfly's painted wings on the tarlatan ballet dress stuck to the chiffon. The music played on relentlessly it seemed, for a child at one end of the scarves took *both*. There was no alternative but for her partner to do likewise, or Pavlova would have been entangled— hence the second child's chagrin. But Madame soon comforted her, saying, ' A'right, darling . . . you clever girl drop one

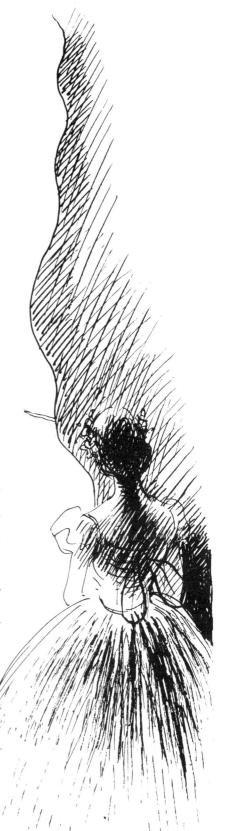

scarf at footlights, you see me I take him round my shoulders after solo. All happy now. *You* know, *I* know, but Press not know, publique not know. A'right, you good girl have some tea.'

She seems to be there still to that grateful child, her eyes bright with loving kindness.

What *was* she like to look at ? It is such a difficult question to answer. She was not a great beauty in the classical sense. It is the eyes that are most remembered, but the whole being was one of loveliness. When Heine, the German poet, was asked were the French women beautiful, he replied, ' Who thinks of the cannon when the ball's hit you ? '

A fraction—a tiny fraction—of the old magic has been captured by the film ; but photographs are at best somewhat dead things, and in those early days were by no means what they are now. Yet a few of them catch something of her spark, and those who never saw her in life can realise what artists meant when going into raptures over her sense of line. The unique personality comes through and certain moments really thrill. Lighting was inadequate, the music not always synchronised with the action ; there is no *décor* worth mentioning, and there were not colour films in those days.

When, however, did such things matter with Pavlova? She appeared to make all as she danced. A famous musician once deplored her choice of composers—until he had seen her. Then he agreed that she could use any music she liked as long as she danced. *Décor* was another almost unnecessary embellishment, for one only saw Pavlova—it was impossible to take one's eyes off her.

To the many whose view of Pavlova had been mostly from the gallery the film was able to give a very welcome closer view of the dancer's technique. Precious details that could be lost or register a little vaguely when so far distant, were now clearly to be seen, and an invaluable lesson to a dancer.

For who could really dissect Pavlova's 'live' dancing? Again and again students would determine to note exactly every move she made and what it was. But then Pavlova began to dance—and the feat was impossible.

It was not that the choreography was especially intricate or complicated. Her solos were comparatively simple in plan and dance arrangement. It should have been easy to recall the routine of steps after

the performance. Was it? No. Snatches maybe, one might recall, not the whole. Note-books were ready, pencils poised, Pavlova danced—and the accessories were discarded. Pavlova herself was all that one could ever see or remember.

' Enchantment ' is an overworked word today, but that is what it was.

J
.921
P338M
c.1

PAVLOVA, ANNA
May
   The Swan

Tillamook County Library
Tillamook, Oregon